HOT OFF THE PRESS

MODERN DAY PARABLES

Dr. Laura Church McCray

HOT OFF THE PRESS "MODERN DAY PARABLES"

Published by BHSB Publishing Company — Dr. Brenda Hawkins Bailey & Steven Bailey Sr.

All scripture quotations taken from the Holy Bible, King James Version of the Bible.

Definitions were gathered from Google/ Webster Dictionary

Book cover designed by BHSB Publishing Company and created by Dr. Brenda Bailey and Dr. Laura Tutu

Editing by Dr. Brenda Hawkins Bailey & Steven Bailey Sr. of BHSB Publishing Company
Printed in the United States of America

ISBN# 979-8-218-98399-4
Library of Congress Control Number on File
Credits

BHSB PUBLISHING COMPANY

Dedication

To my Children and Grand Children: Ebonni, Treyton, Joniah, Elijah, Charles III, Tanyiah, Reaniah, Treyton Jr., Tristan, London,
and Kyran!

I love you all beyond measure!

To My Special Friends: Delphine Booker, Angela Harris, Dr. Brenda Bailey aka Dr. BB, Krystal Lull, Marcia Russell, and Aleisha Crockett, Michael Stevenson

To My Cousins: Latasha Williams and Laletta Davis
Thank you all for supporting me in all my endeavors and whenever I need you.

Table of Parables

Table of Parables

PREFACE

Years ago, when the Lord first saved me, one of my dear friends took me and another friend to a restaurant close to our church. While there he challenged us to come up with "sermon" or topic based on the things we saw in the restaurant. He picked up a bottle of ketchup and tipped it upside down until one drop of ketchup hit the plate. My friend then started preaching about "the blood of Jesus", and how we "only needed one drop" to get the deliverance we needed. From that day to this one, I am always looking for a "PREACH" out of the various activities and occurrences throughout my day.

I started writing "HOT OFF THE PRESS from the desk of L22CM" in the book "FB". People would inbox me and say "you need to compile these and write a book.... you always have the best analogies and parables".

So, here we are!

Most of the parables in this book came from revelations of events that the Lord dropped in my spirit after the events occurred. The thoughts usually came after an event that was unsettling, unusual, inconvenient, or troublesome. God is so amazing, and I love him for teaching me and providing me valuable lessons throughout my experiences. It is my pleasure to share them with you.

FOREWORD

I would like to thank my friend and sister in Christ, Dr. Laura Church McCray affectionately known as Dr. Tutu for choosing me to write the foreword to her first of many books. I am excited and honored to accept this task. Dr. Tutu and I met on the set of the movie "STILLGOTJOY" in which she played a nurse. Not knowing that she was an actual nurse, and her spirit was so enlightening, and we had a blessed encounter. We took photos, laughed, and joked around. I started to watch her Facebook Lives more and discovered she was so encouraging and not afraid to share the word of God with people from all walks of life with no judgement. We call it "the no judgement zone"

The pandemic hit and she being a seamstress as well began to make mask and other paraphernalia to keep us safe. I was like "God it's something about Laura, please show me where or what are we supposed to do to enhance the kingdom together" I supported her business, and we began to speak often. Moving forward a little bit God gave me a show entitled "Gurl Chat With A Twist" to inspire his people during the pandemic, a safe place to share if you will. Before I got the go ahead to do my show I prayed and asked God who should be connected and the first name was Laura Tutu. I approached her and she said yes.

Listen, Laura can take any situation out of her life or others and turn it into a parable to make it make sense. I encouraged her to write a book, but she was already working on one. Then God showed me who she was and how we could enhance the kingdom together "Gurl Chat With A Twist" Dr. Tutu is an amazing Co-Host, and she is an Ambassador for "Gurl Go Get Your Stuff". Her family and I connected in a way that is truly loving, her sons and her daughter are extra special to me. Laura is a great influencer and a team player. Laura is a loyal friend and most of the time she puts others needs before her own.

In this book "Hot Off The Press" Modern Day Parables Dr. Tutu is teaching us through everyday life situation with parables. Most of the parables in this book came from revelations of events that the Lord dropped into her spirit after the events occurred. God is amazing, and Laura will share some of these valuable lessons in this book with you.

Happy Reading,
Dr. Brenda Hawkins Bailey aka Dr.BB

Parable 1

Pour and Stay Full

Your "NOT ANYTHING" is EVERYTHING

Scripture Reference: 2Kings 4:2-6 (NJV)

Are you feeling Empty, Unfulfilled, Without Vision and Void of Purpose? I have felt that way many, many times in my life as well. I have woken up, after a GREAT, POWERFUL day of service the day before; EMPTY! I had to ask myself, what happened between Yesterday and Today? Gee-whiz!

The scripture reminds us in **2Kings 4:2-6 (NJV)** of the lady that thought she had nothing, "NOT ANYTHING" to offer or present for kingdom business. "2) and Elisha said unto her, what shall I do for thee? Tell me, what has thou in the house? And she said, Thine handmaid hath (not anything) in the house, save a pot of oil" **#NOTANYTHING."** Verse 5) reads "so she went from him and shut the door upon her and upon her sons, who brought the vessels to her, and she poured out. 6). And it came to pass, when the vessels were full, that she said unto her son, Bring me yet a vessel. And he said unto her, there is not a vessel anymore. And the OIL STAYED. It's the "And the OIL STAYED" for me.

CONTINUE TO POUR so you can STAY FULL...

#andtheoilstayed

For some of you, this is not the time to stop ministering, to stop preaching and to stop being concerned.

1John 3 (KJV)reminds us “Don’t let your bowels of compassion wax cold”.

Often, we are so consumed with “our own stuff” that we fail to do and perform our assignments. Reminder: our assignments are not hinged upon everything going right in our lives, or if we feel like doing it.

1Peter4: 12-13 (NJV) lets us know “12 Beloved, think it not strange concerning the fiery trial, which is to try you, as though some strange thing happened unto you: 13: But rejoice, inasmuch as ye are partakers of Christ’s sufferings: that, when his glory shall be revealed, ye may be glad also with exceeding joy.

Bottom Line is: “SOME” of you are empty because you STOPPED POURING!

You may feel broken, empty and like “I have nothing to give, and no supply” ...but that could be so very far from the truth...

I remember after having my Hysterectomy, I was depressed, In pain, and just “down and out”. My sister friend called me and said, “is there a word from the Lord today”. I replied, “I have nothing today”. My sister friend said emphatically, “DIG DEEPER, something is in there, and you have to pour it out”. That word and declaration forced me out of my dry, pitiful place, I dug and dug until I struck oil! Silver and Gold had I none, but I HAD SOMETHING!

You have something to off and something to give.... Acts 3 shares a verse where the disciples met a man with what he thought he wanted...It is revealed that They had what he needed. "Silver and Gold have I none, but such as what I do have" ... They had the word for... In God's word, there is life!

The Takeaway

Some of you are FILLED, RE-FILLED and FULFILLED when you are serving the Lord. And you have what people NEED! Your "NOT ANYTHING" is someone else's "EVERYTHING."

#UNTILYOUDORIGHTBYME.... In my (Ms. Celie voice)

SELAH

Prayer

Dear Lord, thank you for allowing me to hear from you today. I pray that the WORD harasses me in my daily comings and goings. Father God, I love you and praise you. Thank you for your word that is so readily available to us for our correction, for our building, for our perfection. Lord, please help me to retain what I have learned today and spit out what is not for me. I want you to be pleased with my life. Father God, Get the glory out of everything that I say and do, in the mighty name of Jesus. Amen!

~TAKE AWAY NOTES~

Parable 2

LEADERS! Now more than ever-LEAD

Scripture Reference: Isaiah 9:16 (KJV) Philippians 2:12 (KJV) 1 Corinthian 9:9(KJV) Acts 20:28(KJV) Mathew 18:6(KJV) Proverbs 16:12(KJV)

Some of us have caused the young saints or the (affectionately known) as the babies to ERR, Backslide, and leave the faith all together. **Isaiah 9:16(KJV) For the leaders of this people cause them to err, and they that are led of them are destroyed**.

Not just Pastors either!!! Anyone declaring to be a leader in any capacity.

Being a LEADER implies that you have FOLLOWERS, because if a person is a "leader" and has no followers, he or she is just a person taking a walk.

You may LEAD in your church, the school, the workplace, or All of the Above. You may drive a bus, teach dance, or coach a team. If you have people following you or emulating what you are doing- YOU ARE A LEADER!

Some may say "I'm not responsible for others, I'm only responsible for myself? And they may even reference the scripture: **Philippians 2:12 (KJV)**that declares "seek your own salvation..." and that is word; however, who would leave a natural baby to clean themselves, prepare their own meals, and provide clothing and shelter? Especially after they have given birth to that baby or taken part in their case.

***DCS would be on the case.**

We are not only accountable behind the pulpit because the World is OUR PULPIT! Our Jobs, our homes, stores, traffic, wherever we frequently visit. (our congregation)

The babies (followers) have looked to you for guidance as they were building their own relationship with God in a greater way. They came to us for Prayer, Comfort, and Guidance. We have Broken them, injured them, and maimed them, sometimes without meaning to; however, whether an injury occurs by accident or on purpose-it must HEAL.

It's Time to Make it Right!

The Takeaway

Repent not only to God but to them! We all have been going through, that's no excuse to Neglect and Abandon your seed!

Negative Attitudes

Backbiting

Manipulation

Stealing and Deceiving

Sexual Immortality

And more...

Isaiah 9:16 (KJV) For the leaders of these people cause them to Err; and they that are led of them are destroyed.

1Corinthian 8:9 (KJV) But take heed lest by any means this liberty of yours become a stumbling block to them that are weak.

Acts 20:28 (KJV) Pay careful attention to yourselves and to all the flock, in which the Holy Spirit has made you overseers to care for the church of God, which he obtained with his own blood.

Matthew 18:6 (KJV) But whoever causes one of these little ones who believe in me to sin, it would be better for him to have a great millstone fastened around his neck and to be drowned in the depth of the sea.

Proverbs 16:12 (KJV) It is an abomination for kings to commit wicked acts, for a throne is established on righteousness.

Prayer

Dear Lord, thank you for allowing me to hear from you today. I pray that the WORD harasses me in my daily comings and goings. Father God, Thank you for your word, and your correction. We don't want to injure anyone by abandoning them, mistreating them, or operating in offense. Help us to take heed to your warnings, and to REPENT swiftly. We love you and want to go back with you when you come! In the name of Jesus. Amen!

Parable 3

When the Healing Takes!

Transparent Moment. Truth Speaks

Scripture Reference: Romans 12:2 (KJV)

The bible reminds us to be so very careful not to be *Easily Offended, Give Offense*, or *Operate in Offense*...It is said that root cause of Offense is insecurity. The Dictionary defines insecurity as: "uncertainty or anxiety about oneself; and/ or lack of confidence". I personally walked in offense, was very easily offended, and did not mind offending others. I had a childhood that fostered "insecurity"; however, even though I could pinpoint the cause of my insecurity, it was ULTIMATELY my responsibility to SEEK, RECEIVE and WALK IN MY HEALING!

So that means I had to get my inside RIGHT and work on ME!

Some of us put on a "good show" and we "FAKE IT UNTIL WE MAKE IT", but the good news is, we don't have to keep faking it! We can walk in freedom and healing. Too much blood was shed on the cross for us to walk around with a measure of relief and Not FREEDOM!

I had all performances of being HEALED and UN-OFFENDED "mastered" outwardly, but NOW it's taken ROOT INWARDLY

I'm going to love you whether you love me or not.

I might even mess around and be genuinely nice to you even when you are not nice to me, because I really desire to.

I may support you when you have never/or stopped your support of me, cause WHO I AM is not really hinged upon who you are to me...NOW that is God! YEP!

Testimony

One day, not too long ago, I had an ought with someone, and I had let bitterness set in and grow in my heart. I prayed and fasted to have this removed. So, I put it to the test lol. I spoke to that someone, and there was NO more pain there-NONE! I WAS FREE! Just saying.

I was singing "CHANGE ME OH GOD" in my T. Mann Voice

A wonderful change has come over me.

The Takeaway

While the blood is running warm in your veins-YOU CAN CHANGE, with the help of the Lord. If you really want to. If you don't like something about yourself, you don't have to have a meeting about it. The world will make you feel justified in walking with HATE AND MALICE in your heart, but we as blood washed believers don't operate by the world's standards!

DO SOMETHING ABOUT IT!

Humble yourself, work on yourself, show yourself Grace, and LOVE YOURSELF. When you know that you know who you are and Whose you are, it is not as easy to get tripped up.

Romans 12:2(KJV) And be not conformed to this world but be ye transformed by the renewing of your mind, that ye may prove what is that good, and acceptable, and perfect will of God.

Prayer

Dear Lord, thank you for allowing me to hear from you today. I pray that the WORD harasses me in my daily comings and goings. God, we sure do thank you for your forgiving, Grace towards us. We thank you for another opportunity to get things right, to walk in forgiveness, and do things your way! Help us to get situations right quickly and according to your word. We love you and believe you to do it! In the name of Jesus. Amen!

~TAKE AWAY NOTES~

Parable 4

It is Well

The World in Rotation-CYCLES

Scripture Reference: Proverbs 3:5-6 ,2Kings 4:22-26 (KJV)

Some Days you feel "ON TOP OF THE WORLD" and other days, you feel like "THE WORLD IS ON TOP OF YOU".

Life Situations, Hormones, aging, and walking through the "Valley of the Shadow of Death" can be taxing and trying of one's faith. The Daily challenges can CONTEND, wrestle, and fight you at your core for your PEACE!

But I have grown to know and trust the Lord more and more!!!

Even when things, situations, and dreams are not only "SEEMINGLY" dead but "COLD-STIFF-STANKIN-and DEAD" ...wooooo glory. God is Fully ABLE to REVIVE, RESTORE, and ATONE!

I "feel" lonely and alone, regretful, and doubtful, sad, and confused at times, just like many others, but and I mean a BIG OLE BUT,

I'm reminded of the scripture in the bible **1Kings 17 (KJV)**...of the widow has found her son dead. HE IS DEAD! But She REMINDED HERSELF of the same God that gave her, her son (using the man of God) and that GOD is alive and well! Elijah came spoke life... and LIFE SHOWED UP.

Another woman lost her son in

2 Kings (KJV) She did not go to the prayer partner this time, she did not have a cheerleading or "Jesus Jesus

Jesus" tarrying squad, she did not go to the altar for Prayer……. *Quickens

She encouraged HERSELF in this fact, "IF GOD, DID IT BEFORE, HE CAN DO IT AGAIN" and Ultimately "IT IS WELL" **2Kings 4:22-26 (KJV)** (read the entire chapter) 26 Run now I pray thee, to meet her, and say unto her, is it well with thee? Is it well with thy husband? Is it well with the child? And she answered, **it is Well**.

The Takeaway

My Brothers and Sisters, don't let the adjectives (the description) of situations or the perspectives and reports of others, make you double the promises of God. This is what the Lord showed me!

Salvation, Faith, and Love are not based on Feelings and Emotions. You must know that you know and WALK IN OUT, SPEAK LIFE.

IT IS WELL!

I felt like Paul when he told King Agrippa, I thought myself happy on this morning!

Prayer

Dear Lord, thank you for allowing me to hear from you today. I pray that the WORD harasses me in my daily comings and goings. Dear Lord. We love you and give you all the Glory. Lord, please forgive us when we did not trust you, did not believe you, and did not put your name on the situation. We thank you for the opportunity to look again, to believe again, and to move forward towards your promises. Glory to God who always causes us to triumph. Help me to hold fast to your word and your instructions. In the name of Jesus. Amen!

~THE TAKEAWAY NOTES~

Parable 5

"BUTT NUGGETS"

Pasteurized or Fresh. That is the question.

Scripture Reference: Matthew 22:14 Leviticus 10:10 (KJV)

I had a coworker bring some farm-fresh eggs from her chickens that are allowed to roam freely and partake in nature and eat when they are hungry-FREE. She affectionately called the eggs from her chickens, "BUTT NUGGETS". She often expressed the love for her chickens, and she enjoyed sharing their eggs with her co-workers. The egg cartons she sent me were borrowed from another set of eggs. Each egg was a slightly different shade and size. There were no carbon copies of the other ones in that container. My store-bought ones on the other hand were all bright white, same size, and had a cute little red stamp on them. The RED STAMP signified that the eggs all had me someone's standard.

One Saturday morning I woke up and my little Honey Bun, Chaz, asked if I could prepare him a good breakfast. I mixed 2 store bought eggs (with the red stamp) on them in a bowl. I scrambled and mixed them up beautifully, but I needed more eggs to feed us both. I grabbed 2 of the "farm fresh" "free range" eggs, the BUTT NUGGETS. To my surprise, the RED STAMP eggs and the Butt nuggets were difficult to mix together.

The yolks of the BUTT NUGGETS were bright yellow and firmer than those of the RED STAMP eggs. The yolks of the different eggs did not want to break down and blend. Mixing the eggs required a lot of manipulation and work.

The Takeaway

Sometimes people in the church get so conditioned and traditionalized that they lose the Originality, the Zeal, and the Individualism that God has given them, JUST TO MEET SOMEONE'S STANDARD. They blend in, appear, and behave just like all the other "eggs". The bible lets us know that many are the called "for many are called, but few are chosen" Matthew 22:14 (KJV)It is not wrong to be in a crowd, but you don't want to become "the Crowd". You are called to stand out, and not "FIT IN". And when God has called you out to be different, YOU PUT A DIFFERENCE. Leviticus 10:10. (KJV) Sometimes you must not only come from among THEM (the sinners), but also THEM (the saints).

Prayer

Dear Lord, thank you for allowing me to hear from you today. We pray that the WORD harasses us in our daily comings and goings. WE want to please you with our lives. Please help us to retain the revelations you give us. Help us to be original and not so entangled in others that we don't hear you. We desire to be used by you and to grow the kingdom of God. In Jesus' mighty name. Amen.

~TAKE AWAY NOTES~

Parable 6

"Sticks and Stones"

Words have Power

Scripture Reference: Proverbs 18:21 (KJV)

I remember the day the Lord Placed this in my spirit. "Sticks and Stones may break my bones, but words can never hurt me". But don't sleep on the power of received words!

I don't receive any word curses, ill thoughts, manipulative blurt outs, foolish gestures, or anything else that is NOT OF GOD! **#returntoSENDER...**

Proverbs 18:21 (KJV) Death and life are in the power of the tongue: and they that love it shall eat the fruit thereof.

Many of us have been called all kinds of names down through the years. All the colorful words: cat, rat, dog, fool, and other 4letter words. But we don't answer to names that our mothers and God did not give us. We don't respond to damning curses and plots and plans of the enemy!

This came to mind...

Daniel did not answer to name Belteshazzar, the name King Nebuchadnezzar called him, nor did he participate in the traditions of his captivity. He hung on to the WORDS and plans that were laid out for him by his God. He chose not to be overcome by circumstances and what "he saw" and was even threatened with. Daniel stood on what he believed, and he stayed True to the Things of His God.

Another example:

My guy Hezekiah was told some "words" that told him to get his house in order. He was warned that his life was soon to end. Hezekiah refused to receive those words! Instead, he turned his face to the wall and kept the Lord in remembrance of HIS WORD. Hezekiah reminded the Lord how he had obeyed and done the things assigned to his hands. Who is in your ear? Who are you listening to? Whose Report will you believe?

The Takeaway

I encourage you to SPEAK LIFE and God's WORDS over yourself. Stop receiving everything that is said to you. Try it against the word of God. Revisit the promises that God has made to you in his word, and through other servants that he has used to speak life into you. Go back and look at words you have written down.

LOOK AGAIN! And BELIEVE AGAIN. Don't go by what you see, go by what God said!

Prayer

Dear Lord, thank you for allowing me to hear from you today. I pray that the WORD harasses me in my daily comings and goings. Father God, I love you and praise you. Thank you for your word that is so readily available to us for our correction, for our building, for our perfection. Lord, please help me to retain what I have learned today and spit out what is not for me. I want to be pleased with my life. Help me to always speak life over myself and others and reject any word curses, or anything else that comes to cancel out the promises. The devil is a Liar! Father God, Get the glory out of everything that I say and do, in the mighty name of Jesus. Amen!

~TAKE AWAY NOTES~

Parable 7

"A" Remnant

There is an Army Rising up.

Scripture Reference: Psalm 105:5 Jeremiah 1:5 (KJV)

We as believers continue to hear about the group of people that are coming to the Lord, the ones that will preach revival, and the ones that WILL NOT LOOK OR BEHAVE LIKE US! And I believe it. WE hear this said and sung often. "there's an Arm Rising Up", and they won't be walking, talking, dressing, dancing, singing, or serving Like you or me!

I was chatting with my dear sister the other day. We were discussing the JUDGEMENTALNESS of people, and the UNATTRACTIVENESS of our current "CHURCH".

We visited the scripture Psalm 105:5 (KJV)which admonishes us to "touch not my anointing..." So many of the "saints" have been trained on What "anointing look likes" and what "Holiness" looks like...and use those stipulations and characteristics to decide if someone is "anointed "or "saved" as a result. WE ARE OUT HERE TOUCHING ER THANG and EVERYONE?

Please Go back and Read that Again!

***Listen-I have been guilty of this very thing. I thank God for the Pandemic and the teaching I have received from the Holy Spirit.

I remember a story I heard about a man coming into a Pre-school and letting the faculty know that there was a student that would one day become the president of the USA. Understandably, the teachers all wanted to know who the student was. The man said, "the Lord did not tell me to give you that information, because he wants you to treat them all as if they are the student that would be a President one day".

What are you saying Laura? We don't really know what the "anointing" looks like, or who has accepted the Lord as their savior, or will come into their calling from God, or who has come into the knowledge and in "right" relationship with God but does not LOOK LIKE what we think they should look like. Everyone was formed in their mothers' bellies and already have a call on their lives. Jeremiah 1:5 (KJV)says: "Before I formed thee in the belly, I knew thee; and before thou camest forth out of the womb I sanctified thee, and I ordained thee a prophet unto the nations". Whatever they are or will be is there, and you may just not be able to see it.

The Takeaway

It would be great practice to Treat everyone as if they have a calling on their lives, and the calling may have not manifested yet.... or quite possible has manifested. You just don't recognize it. Many of these Soldiers are still being groomed for Greatness, still healing from Trauma, and still Hearing assignments, and they may be confused by the communication. Woo my sisters and brothers, just wait for it!

There are some who will never walk in the knowledge of the truth, and guess what? WE have to love them too, even when they don't love us.

There are many people out here "doing the work" of evangelist, missionaries, ministers, "SAINTS" and have never taken the right hand of fellowship. Help us, Lord.

#noShadeonAnyoneElse

There's an Army Rising up.

Prayer

Dear Lord, thank you for allowing me to hear from you today. I pray that the WORD harasses me in my daily comings and goings. I want to please you with my life. Please help me to retain the revelations you give me. I desire to be used by you to grow the kingdom of God. I desire to love everyone and treat them as I would treat myself. In Jesus mighty name.

Amen!

~TAKE AWAY NOTES~

Parable 8

I am an Encourager!

Scripture Reference: 1Thessalonians 5:11 Deuteronomy 31:6(KJV)

Are you a person that wants to make sure people know when they have done something wrong, or something that has "rubbed you the wrong way?" Do you fill out comment cards? ask for the manager or call back to report negative events? Have you ever considered that you are a light? You can say one thing to change the situation, turn someone's life around. You can even change the trajectory of a person's circumstances with your Encouragement! You could take "that same energy" and bless someone with it, even if it doesn't make sense to do it..." they don't deserve it"- Do IT ANYWAY!

In other news...

The Takeaway

People can know stuff about you and even admire stuff about you, but their own stubbornness, jealousy or insecurities will keep them from watering and speaking into your life. Those same people will pour salt and throw shade when your name comes up, but who cares? What God has for you is for you! Maybe what you just read describes you. It certainly describes a season of my life. If it applies to you-repent, stop it, and start being an ENCOURAGER. First encourage yourself, and then it will spread to others. It is so much more rewarding, empowering and fulfilling. So going forward,

COMPLIMENT YOURSELF!!!

SPEAK OVER YOURSELF!

Stop competing with others, and only compete with yesterday's YOU! And others realizing it won't take anything from you.

I have said this before, and you may see it again as you read this book to parables.

*** Know that you know that you know that you know...Who you are and Whose you are!!! Beautifully and Wonderfully Made! Now Go and Be Great in God!!

#IamAnENCOURAGER

Prayer

Dear Lord, thank you for allowing me to hear from you today. I pray that the WORD harasses me in my daily comings and goings. Dear Lord, please help us to stop worrying about if people celebrate with us and help us to START encouraging and celebrating others. Father God, we want to represent you with the Love that you have for us and share that other, even when they don't want it or in our eyes deserve it. Thank you for this reminder. We want to please you. In the name of Jesus, Amen!

Parable 9

TRANSITIONS

You are Changing.

Scripture Reference: Romans 8:28 2Corinthians 5:17 (KJV)

Sometimes when you are transitioning levels, you are actively Being BIRTHED (not giving birth), but YOU are the BABY-The Creation. You are the one that is being developed, being molded, and shaped into a NEW CREATURE and into a NEW PLACE.

During transitioning, it gets DARK, it can get uncomfortable, LONELY, the living quarters can get tight, and quite frankly you may even boo boo, "take a dump" (defecate) where you live, and THAT PLACE starts

STANKIN!!!

Defecating in the womb is a sign that the BABY is getting too Big for that space and has OUTGROWN that place and Transitioning is Near! In this walk there are MANY TRANSITIONS from GLORY TO GLORY!

Human Anatomy shares with us that the baby's skull and other bones have to become out of alignment, become somewhat deformed in order to fit in such a space as a tubular womb before TRUE ALIGNMENT and TRANSFIGURATION can take place. Once "BORN" the care providers and the parent will rub the skull bones and place a baby cap on the baby's tiny little head to help promote shaping, but ultimately the head will take proper shape...my my my Good God from Zion! Thank you, Holy Ghost!

Can anyone Relate?

The Take-Away

You may be in a place that you have been in for a long time. People are starting to get on your nerves, it is a task to continue to "SHOW UP" for you or anyone else. You feel trapped and uncomfortable. Maybe just Maybe you are in the Proverbial "NINTH MONTH" of your development and it's time to be BORN into a new situation! Maybe you are literally in the birthing canal-you're experiencing "spiritual headaches" "pulling" and "pushing" from other sources. It doesn't feel good but remember, Romans 8:28 (KJV) All things (the good things, the bad things) ALL THINGS are working for OUR GOOD! 2 Corinthians 5:17 (KJV) says "Therefore, if anyone is in Christ, the new creation has come." #Transition #NeverGraduate

Transition can be uncomfortable. EMBRACE CHANGE.

Prayer

Dear Lord, thank you for allowing me to hear from you today. I pray that the WORD harasses me in my daily comings and goings. Father God, I love you and praise you. Thank you for your word that is so readily available to us for our correction, for our building, for our perfection. Lord, please help me to retain what I have learned today and spit out what is not for me. Help me to embrace the changes that you are allowing to take place in my life. I know it is for my good. I want you to be pleased with my life. Father God, get the glory out of everything that I say and do, in the mighty and matchless name of Jesus. Amen!

~TAKE AWAY NOTES~

Parable 10

Are you COMMUNICATING or just TALKING?

Scripture Reference: Proverbs 4:7 (KJV)

Communication: the impar/ting or exchanging of information or news

Communication is only effective if the one receiving actually RECIEVES! A person can be "really deep", "highly educated" and be very knowledgeable in a particular area, but if they cannot regurgitate the information in a way that the hearers can received and understand—DID COMMUNICATION TAKE PLACE?

Here is an example of a time when communication was attempted but failed.

Example 1.

I was sent a text message from a phone company years ago. The text was sent in a language that I don't speak or read. In the message, I recognized a monetary amount. Because I don't speak the other language, I immediately thought it was a bill. I proceeded to call a phone company and I became furious, I thought to myself "I don't own them anything". I called the phone service and insisted that I did not owe anything. The representative informed me that I had been given a CREDIT, and the message was sent to me in that Language by mistake.

***Sometimes we talk to people WAY over their heads because "we have studied", and "we have revelation" for many reasons. We want people to know how smart we are, or how much we have studied, but again, HAS COMMUNICATION TAKEN PLACE??

Jesus spoke in Parables for this Very Reason!

Here is an example of knowing a lot but being able to get on the "level" of the hearer to actually COMMUNICATE effectively.

Example 2.

I was in nursing school years ago and I struggled in the Cardiac portion of school. I asked my professors to explain the blood flow of the heart, chambers, arteries, veins, and electricity. The professor continued to reference the textbook (which was not wrong); however, me as a novice student could not fully understand what it was trying to communicate. I asked a very Prominent cardiologist in Murfreesboro to explain the process in more detail. This humble cardiologist (and good friend) who is an "EXPERT" DEEP IN SUBJECT MATTER, could have gotten all "EXTRA DEEP" with his explanation-because this is his area of expertise. Instead, he drew a cartoon heart and cartoon arrows, and gave analogies and examples, and talked to me in very simple verbiage and actually COMMUNICATED the facts and TAUGHT me what I needed to learn.

HE HAD NOTHING TO PROVE!

This style of teaching was not him "dummying down" the information, but rather meeting the needs of the person that needed to learn. That TAKES MORE!

The Takeaway

When you FULLY understand the Matters which you are trying to teach you can make it easy for the listener to grasp! Otherwise, you are just talking. If you don't understand something that someone is trying to communicate to you- ASK QUESTIONS. There is NO dumb question. Also, let me add. It doesn't matter if everyone else in the room understands the information. ASK!

Prayer:

Dear Lord, thank you for allowing me to hear from you today. I pray that the WORD Harasses me in my daily comings and goings. I want to please you with my life. Please help me to retain the revelations you give me. I pray for strategic ways to reach people through effective communication, to get on their levels where they may understand. I desire to be used by you to grow the kingdom of God, in Jesus' mighty name. Amen!

~TAKE AWAY NOTES~

____

____

____

____

____

____

Parable 11

NOT MY BATTLE

"and Battles we do not have to Fight"

Scripture Reference: Isaiah 22:22 Matthew 16:19 Hebrews 10:35-36 (KJV)

One morning, I came into work from the parking lot. I went for my ear buds so I could make a call before logging in. My earbud case was not on my keychain.

*My keychain has a little pocket on it that houses my license (ID), and a few other cards that I keep for quick access.

I made my call, holding the phone and I clocked in as I do every morning. I never noticed my keys were gone. I called into the office, and was talking to my BOSS and an officer called TRYING TO FIND ME.

My boss gave me an ACCESS CODE to call the OFFICER back. I called him and he told me "I have your KEYS, that you lost SOME HOW". The officer went on to say, "you sure are lucky". He then asked, "what is with your keys". I told him the contents of my keychain/wallet, and he replied, "I did an inventory, and everything is STILL HERE".

Isaiah 22:22 reads "22 I will place on his shoulder the key to the house of David; what he opens no one can shut, and what he shuts no one can open".

I will give you the keys of the kingdom of Heaven, and whatever you bind on earth shall have been bound in heaven, and whatever you loose on earth shall have been loosed in heaven.

The enemy comes to try and steal, kill, and destroy: Your life, Your identity, Your purpose, Your family, Your promises, Your Destiny, and Your Keys! OOOOh But when you have the Blessed assurance and Jesus is your Lord and you are His-He will allow you to RECOVER ALL, even that which you had *NO IDEA WAS EVER LOST!*

You will win Battles that you did not even know you were fighting.

~TAKE AWAY NOTES~

Parable 12

"Who wouldn't serve a God like this? "Scripture Reference: Galatian 5:22-23 Matthew 5:3-12 (KJV)

Many of us have magnificent Testimonies. We can't fathom how someone would not run to the altar screaming "what must I do to be saved?", "how can I have what you have?".

Well. A lot of people would not serve a God like our because some of our attributes that we choose to let show and override the Fruits of the Spirit:

Our NEGATIVE ATTITUDES

Our POOR DISPOSITIONS

Our DEFEATED CONVERSATIONS

Our TEMPER TANTRUMS

We are the RE-presentation of Jesus Christ to the hurting, hopeless, and dying world and some of us blend right in with our behavior, our dress code, our speech and so on...

Review the List Above

The Takeaway

PRESENTATION is everything! Let someone bring your plate of foot out with juices running all into each other and just not looking right... You may be reluctant to eat it! But it may be delicious and very healthy. But the presentation is a hinderance.

People say, “I don’t care what nobody say about me”, “I’m living my Best Life.” Well, as a Blood Washed believer- YOU SHOULD, and your best life should present Jesus to the World-Verbally and Nonverbally!

“Actions Speak Louder Than Words”

soul, and all your spirit and it will SHOW UP ON THE OUTSIDE. “Catch on fire and the whole world will come watch you Burn.”

Prayer

Dear Lord, thank you for allowing me to hear from you today. I pray that the WORD harasses me in my daily comings and goings. I want to please you with my life. Please help me to retain the revelations you give me. Help me with my attitude, my disposition, my conversation, my tantrums, my words, and my demeanor. Please help me to represent you in a greater way. In Jesus’ name. Amen!

~TAKE AWAY NOTES~

Parable 13

WRITE THEN RUN

"Cart before Horse"

Scripture Reference: Habakkuk 2 (KJV)

Some of us stay on the Go! We are willing to do tasks, and we are physically able to "do the tasks", but we lack all the ingredients to accomplish the assignments. The ingredients can include understanding, provision, and assistance etc. It is like the verbiage, "putting the cart before the horse". I have been SO guilty of "PUTTING THE CART BEFORE THE HORSE" and writing the vision and RUNNING without waiting on the PLAIN" part to manifest...

Habakkuk 2:2(KJV)

"2 **And the Lord answered me, and said, Write the vision, and make it plain upon tables, that he may run that readeth it."**

As a Result of moving haste fully, and before season, I have had some pre-mature births in many situations.
In some cases, I have lost some of "my babies", and opportunities for conception...and in other case the babies survived but required more attention, cost more, and sometimes didn't reach maximum potential as maybe they would have had they come forth to full term.
**** But on Today! I have the Horse in place, and the "blinkers" are on, and she is ready to ride-WHEN READY

ARRIVES! Ready is Nigh! Get your Horses in the Barn and Saddle up!

Other times we Have the vision and the "ingredients", but we lack drive, and we don't run. While we are dragging our feet and waiting, our ships are sailing and have sailed, and we did not accomplish the assignment placed in our hands. Remember this, if the Lord can't rely on us, he will find and use someone else.

"We WENT, but were we SENT."

The Takeaway

Horse Blinkers, sometimes known as blinders, are a piece of horse tack that prevent the horse from seeing to the rear and in some cases, to the side.... Keeping his eyes on the prize and not being distracted or impatient! There are so many kinds of people in the world. Some are late for everything, "some are right on time for everything, and some are super early for everything". Ask God to help you with Timing, "PLAINESS" and when to Come and Go. If for some reason "you operated out of season" and were distracted by LIFE, Fix it, and move on. KNOWLEDGE IS POWER!

Prayer

Dear Lord, thank you for allowing me to hear from you today. I pray that the WORD harasses me in my daily comings and goings. Thank you for giving me vision, goals, and aspiration. Thank you for giving me people to confirm. Thank you for giving me strength and boldness to carry out your plan. We bind the enemy of our souls, and we bind the draw back spirit. Help us to write the vision, make it plain, and the RUN.

~TAKE AWAY NOTES~

Parable 14

Ministry Starts at Home

Scripture Reference: 1 Timothy 5:8 (KJV)

Ministry absolutely starts at home!!! We should minister, love, teach and nurture our own first!

HOWEVER, in the event that your Family doesn't respond to the Godly teaching, and/or they operate totally contrary to what you have taught them, prayed for them about, and lived before them.

You Still have to operate in Your Calling

You still may Preach about the same thing that "they" are doing.

You still have to Go Forth

You still have to Tune out the folks that don't really know your situation!

And by all means

You still have to keep those Family members up before the Lord! And hold fast to and put a Demand on the promises and the words of the Highest God!

"Charity begins at home" applies to all Christians. The scripture 1Timothy 5:8(KJV) stated, "but if anyone does not provide for his own, and especially for those of his household, he has denied the faith and is worse than an unbeliever.

The Takeaway

No matter WHAT comes or goes, no matter WHO comes or goes, continue to love, nurture, and encourage your HOME and believe God who promised. While you are waiting, plead the blood over your family and continue to do the Will of the Lord.

Prayer

Dear Lord, thank you for allowing me to hear from you today. I pray that the WORD harasses me in my daily comings and goings. Father God, I love you and honor you. I need your strength to minister and serve my Family as you would be pleased with. Please Lord, give me the strength to avoid discouragement when seeing things that are contrary to what you desire. Help me to hold fast to your will concerning me. Thank you for your strength and guidance concerning ministry and service. In Jesus' Name. Amen!

~TAKE AWAY NOTES~

Parable 15

Let God Be your Guide

"THEY"

Scripture Reference: Mark 6:4 Romans 8:1 (KJV)

Many ministers of the Gospel have fallen short and missed "the mark" as it relates to service. We have either omitted to do something or just did something wrong. Other ministers of the gospel can find your "failures" and "mishaps" to be horrible, and they will never see you "RIGHT" again. Sometimes it seems like you can't outlive "what you did", "where you went", and even "who you are". This can leave you feeling like a "lost cause", and the enemy tries to use condemnation, but we will believe the word that declares:

Romans 8:1 (KJV) There is therefore now no condemnation to them which are in Christ Jesus, who walk not after the flesh, but after the Spirit. FORGIVE YOURSELF FRIENDS!

The Takeaway

Your ministry and service didn't stop because "THEY" stopped talking to you.

God did not stop blessing you because "THEY" got mad at you.

The Benediction has not been spoken over you because "THEY" have spoken it over your relationship with them. "THEY" may be able to affect how others respond to you, but "THEY" cannot stop of affect how God responds to you! "THEY" are not that great, grand, and wonderful.

#forgive #rebukeBITTERNESS #avoidOFFENSE and #GOWITHGOD

SELAH

Prayer

Dear Lord, thank you for allowing me to hear from you today. I pray that the WORD harasses me in my daily comings and goings. Father God, we love you and give you glory. Thank you for forgiving us when we sincerely ask. Thank you for another chance to say yes to your will and yes to your way. Thank you for the ability to forgive ourselves. Help us to pick ourselves up and START OVER on the path you have put us on. You have started us on a good work, and you will perform it until the day of Jesus Christ! Thank you thank you Thank you for 1your grace and mercy! I'm excited to please you Lord, In Jesus' Name, Amen

~TAKE AWAY NOTES~

____

____

____

____

____

____

____

____

____

____

Parable 16

Are you better because you met me?

Scripture Reference: Matthew 5:43-45 Matthew 5: 13-16 (KJV)

Ask yourself that question when you meet New People, and the Oldest Acquaintances.

Did I impact this Person in a Positive Way?

You never really know what people are going through! You may assume you do, because of how they carry themselves, and navigate throughout daily activities. Some people won't say a word about their issues; but every now and then they will tell you or they will carry the struggle on their faces. Most of the time, you can't tell that someone has been recently:

BROKEN

BETRAYED

ABUSED

VIOLATED

And/or

STRUGGLING with life's STUFF!

Many are trying to "BE" strong because they know if they "break down" or "spazz out" those around them could potentially be affected do.... "Something about that Energy"

We don't know the STRESS LEVEL that people are operating under. We don't know the breaking point that they may be very close to. Now, I know God can heal and deliver. JESUS IS THE ANSWER, but sometimes, life just takes a toll on a person.

I beseech ye therefore brethren to BE (not act) Nice and good to people-ALL PEOPLE: (strangers, family, friends, and neighbors. Oh, and telemarketers). WE should exhibit these behaviors whether in person, and on the phone. We should say something kind, or just be tolerant with that person that is not so easy to love.

"ITS DEEPER THAN THE NAIL" ... "Yeah, I see the nail, but how in the world did it get there.... there has to be a reason".

Wouldn't it be terrible if you were the person that said that said that one thing and behaved that certain way that was the "straw that broke the camel's back".

The Takeaway

"I WANT THIS PERSON BETTER FOR HAVING MADE MY ACQUAINTANCE TODAY-because I may never see them again". Put your best Face and best Behavior Forward. Represent Christ!

Prayer

Dear Lord, thank you for allowing me to hear from you today. I pray that Your WORD harasses me in my daily comings and goings. Father God, please use me to represent you in a way that brings you pleasure and edifies you to the uttermost, in my home, on my job, in the streets, and the marketplace. Let me say or do something that will uplift people that you have placed in my path and in my life. I don't want anyone to stumble or cry because of Me. Endow me with discernment, that I may see the tears behind the smile. In Jesus' Name, Amen!

~TAKE AWAY NOTES~

Parable 17

What are you Connect to?

"Stay Directly Connected to the Vine"

Scripture Reference: John 15:5 (KJV)

5 "Yes, I am the vine; you are the branches. Those who remain in me, and I in them, will produce much fruit. For apart from me you can do nothing.

Specific attention to vs 5 Remaining "IN" me VS "NEAR" me. Near is equivalent to apart.

Many of us utilize so many devices and often we hook our equipment up to a "BLUE TOOTH" apparatus which allows us to "WANDER" away from the direct source.

Technology allows one to stay "connected" but not directly. You must; however, be "NEAR" the device you are wanting to take advantage of using known as "PAIRING". Now we know this technology has made our lives so much better, so much more convenient...but let's talk about the frustration we have when

"WE CAN NOT CONNECT"

Scenario: you are in the middle of an important conversation, and you get in your car, start it up and during the "transition" from outside to car you lose several key points of the convo! Ugh... "Please say that again, my blue tooth didn't connect".

I don't know about you, but I have been guilty of this spiritually. I have relied on others who were "NEAR" me to keep me informed, to keep me on fire, and to keep me

"CONNECTED", but I really wasn't connected. I was NEAR IT, BUT NOT CONNECTED TO IT! **#closeproximitywontworkinthisstory.**

PAIRING is great for prayer, praising, and patty cake, but with ONE-ON-ONE time with God-YOU MUST BE CONNECTED!

Another Scenario: If you have a device that need charging and you throw the power chord over "by" the outlet, you will REMAIN UNCHARGED, and frustrated.

I know chords and wires can be a nuisance but there is Nothing Like a "LAND LINE" and being "GROUNDED" to the source of POWER--- *quickens

The Takeaway

Get Plugged in and CONNECTED. Don't be satisfied with closeness and being in the same room. GET CONNECTED, get at the Feet of Jesus!

Prayer: Dear Lord, thank you for allowing me to hear from you today. I pray that Your WORD harasses me in my daily comings and goings. Father God, please forgive me for relying on others to FEED me when you taught me how to COOK and find substance in your word. Thank you for this reminder, Lord. My desire is to please you and to get to know you in a greater way! Amen and Amen.

Parable 18

WORDS HAVE POWER

Scripture Reference: 2Timothy 2:15 (KJV)

Backstory:

One of my children was in the newspaper frequently while playing sports and was in the Daily News Journal local paper, quite a bit. Once after a tournament at MTSU, this particular write up said "a DEJECTED...." Bla blab la. After reading that "attack" (so I thought) I immediately took offense, thinking "my child ain't DEJECTED" From lack of knowledge, I thought "he is not REJECTED, he is not DISGUSTED.... he is only Disappointed" ....

I was about to call the paper and express my concerns for the write up, but I halted and took, the liberty of looking the word up first. LOLOLOLOL... it turns out that my child was VERY VERY DEJECTED. His team had lost the championship, and he was upset! which is ultimately what DEJECTED meant.

Many times, we get upset, confused, offended and in trouble because of "lack of knowledge" and "laziness to seek truth". We are saying, repeating, and declaring things that we ourselves don't have full or "ANY" understanding of. We are taking offense or "feeling small" when people who have a vast vocabulary use it on us. #IMTICKLED Word HAVE POWER.

I hear folks out here singing and saying things that they had no idea the meaning of.

***2 Songs come to mind: “my milk shake brings……”, and “APPLY Pressure”. I agree both songs have cool beats, but the lyrics and the meanings of the songs are sketchy and Riske at best. (MY OPINION, MY BOOK). Not trying to be deep.

The bible encourages us to STUDY TO SHOW OURSELVES APPROVED! And one of my fellow church members wrote a poem years ago (while still a child) “IGNORANCE ISNT BLISS” … Both statements let us know that it is up to us, our responsibility to COLLECT, GATHER, AND RETAIN KNOWLEDGE of words, laws, and things around us that can directly or indirectly affect us.

WORDS HAVE POWER.

Furthermore, we shouldn’t get angry or feel smaller when people use words that we don’t know. Rather, we should be challenged to obtain the meaning and learn new words.

Be challenged today to obtain KNOWLEDGE, Learn Different WORDS, and stay in the KNOW.

At very least, look up the words that you don’t know before reacting or responding.

Funny Story: I had a friend whose mother was a sanctified preacher. Several years ago, there was a commercial about a Particular Beer. The commercial had 3 cute frogs that would say the syllables of the drink, but never heard them all together quickly. Frog one said “BUD”. Frog two said “WY”, and Frog three said “ZER”. My friend’s mother had "heard" the commercial several times, while doing other things around the house. One day in the grocery store she started saying "BUD..................WY...................... ZER" over and over again, emulating the frog, Voices. My friend Yelled "MOMMA, what are you saying???" Her mom replied, "what the frogs say on the commercial". My friend told her mother "That's a beer commercial momma". Her mother became red in the face and felt convicted and had a fit...lol. This is comical, but it's just an example of how catchy phrases and songs are, and how that can provoke a person to want to say them too; regardless of having knowledge of meaning. BYE

The Takeaway

Your words have Power, and so do the words of others. Be careful what you allow to enter your ear gates and your spirit. Be slow to speak and careful to listen. Study, Discern and Live!

Prayer

Dear Lord, thank you for allowing me to hear from you today. I pray that Your WORD harasses me in my daily comings and goings. Thank you, father, for giving us so many platforms to collect and retain knowledge. Thank you for the reminder today that words have power....SO MUCH POWER. The enemy desires to trick us and have us say words that could be suggestive, offensive, and dangerous, but we are not ignorant concerning his schemes. Thank you for your forgiving, Grace. In Jesus' Name. Amen.

~TAKE AWAY NOTES~

Parable 19

When you think you have done too Much

"BE FREE"

Scripture Reference: Matthew 18:15-17(KJV)

1Corinthian 10:23 (KJV)

Singing "I gotta clean up what I messed up, start my life over again."

Some people have reconciled relationships and they feel that they can't share the reunion, can't post about it, or enjoy it openly, because they did so much when it was in turmoil, "I don't want to seem like a hypocrite" ... WHO CARES!!!

Well, I want to challenge you to embrace the relationship that the Lord has reunited. If others can't deal with it, then that is THEIR problem-Not yours.

The truth of the matter is that "they" (the same OTHERS that I mentioned above) are probably one of the reasons the relationship fell apart anyway-DIRECT SABBOTAGE. And guess what, we forgive them too!

Some of you may feel "funny" because you too have been guilty of talking about, acting petty and being ugly towards or about the person (that God has brought back in your life) in the presence of others, so you are worried of how you may look. WHO CARES??!!!!! Life is Short.

***Repent**, apologize (to the person and the ones you may have poisoned concerning the person) and ENJOY LIFE and your renewed friendships and relationships. PERIODTT

I said this earlier in the year. "Going forward, I base all of my relationships and encounters on the energy given directly to me, not second hand or left-over energy that someone else shared with me". I will allow the Lord to minister to me concerning who I should allow access to me.

Please don't be that person, that when you have an ought with someone, you want everyone else to have an ought. First of all, DO THE BIBLE, and get your ought taken care of so that you may have production dialogues with the Lord **(GET PRAYERS THROUGH).**

Matthew 18:15-17 (KJV) "if your brother or sister sins, go and point out their fault, just between the two of you. If they listen to you, you have won them over. But if they will not listen, take one or two others along, so that every matter may be established by the testimony of two or three witnesses. If they still refuse to listen, tell It to the church, and if they refuse to listen even to the church, treat them as you would a pagan or a tax collector.

And secondly, if you can't do the WORD, at least don't be a murderer of the brethren. If you don't LOVE, you HATE.

1John 3:15 (KJV)Whoever hates his brother is a murderer, and you know that no murderer has eternal life abiding in him.

I have had several relationships RECONCILED, mended, empowered, renewed, and strengthened THIS YEAR AND IM SO MUCH BETTER FOR IT! Oh, and some, I have cordially moved into another investment bracket!

The Takeaway

If you are a LEADER, please please be careful not to Abuse your power. Your followers are depending on you to lead them correctly, they are hanging on your every word. So be slow to speak and operate at the right time!

1 Corinthians 10:23 (KJV) All things are lawful for me, but all things are not expedient; all things are lawful for me, but all things edify not.

Prayer

Dear Lord, thank you for allowing me to hear from you today. I pray that Your WORD harasses me in my daily comings and goings. Father thank you for reconciliation. Thank you for the opportunity to mend relationships and start afresh. Thank you for giving me the boldness to be humble, honest, and true to myself and you. Help me going forward to make healthy decisions and have holy conversations. I love you for allowing me to grow and represent you in a greater way. In Jesus' Name. Amen!

Parable 20

REBUKE the messenger.

Scripture: 1 Corinthian 13:5 (KJV)

I have a really great friend that has been in my life for over 20 years.
Some leaders/ other friends shared some "tea" with me that the enemy used, and "I allowed" the information to "taint" my opinion of this dear friend. I did not confront the friend, nor did I give that friend the opportunity to share, explain, admit, or deny.
I just put them on trial without them even being there. I then proceeded to share I missed out of several years of great real FRIENDSHIP as a result of that.
Well. Let's cut through the field.

I had major surgery last year and my daughter made a post asking for prayers and such. This same friend (from paragraph one), reached out to me, while he was out of town. He checked on me, sent me money, and stated, "when I get back in town, I'm going to check on you again" AND HE DID!

I had people that I "ROCKED" with every day that did not do what this friend did. 4(four) years of my life came crashing to my remembrance, and the Lord got me all the way together. Sometimes we feel justified in our "disobedience to the word" and our MIS-behavior. The devil is a whole lie.

I asked this friend to "PLEASE FORGIVE ME", this friend did not require any details. This friend forgave me, not only with WORDS but with RESTORED RELATIONSHIP.

Singing: "I'm so happy to see you and me back in stride again"

The Takeaway

The bottom line is even if the "tea" was true (which I don't believe it was, but it doesn't matter) *** the great service of Friendship that has been rendered down through the years should have superseded that one little infraction. And we should never put someone on trial without giving them an opportunity to "BE THERE" especially if it's "YOUR FRIEND". We are allowing relationships to be destroyed over little itty-bitty things.

IM FREE TODAY!

Prayer

Dear Lord, thank you for allowing me to hear from you today. I pray that Your WORD harasses me in my daily comings and goings. Father, I thank you for the spirit of reconciliation. Thank you for allowing me to reunite with people that you have placed in my life for GROWTH and LESSONS. You alone God get the glory for this situation. Continue to fertilize and nurture bonds that will bring you pleasure and that will bring life.

~TAKE AWAY NOTES~

Parable 21

3 Turns Away

Scripture: Proverbs 4:7 (KJV)

In a Back slidden condition, my friend and I went on a "sightseeing drive" with our children. We were dressed like we had rolled out of the bed; our hair was not combed, our car had been wrecked, had a quarter tank of gas, and we had one bar on the cricket phone... A MESS! We both had our children in the car, and they looked just like us... lol We had No business being out in public. During our drive, we talked about the backslidden conditions we were in, and how much wrong we had been doing. We agreed that "we had done way too much for the Lord to FORGIVE US"

While in this Gorgeous neighborhood, comprised of Mansions and beautiful greenery, we realize WE ARE LOST. I told my friend to pull up in this well-lit driveway. She pulled all the way up the driveway; and before we could put the car in park, a little lady came out on the porch. We said, "WE ARE GOING TO JAIL". lol

The Lady said, "can I help you?". We said, "we are lost". She asked, "where do you all live?". We replied, "off of Bell Road". She said, "well you are ONLY 3 TURNS AWAY". Her husband joined her on the porch, and we asked, "why are you up this late?". She said, "we are waiting on our daughter to come home. "My friend and I looked at each other and reflected on our conversation. The Lord started talking and REVEALING!!!

The husband said "turn right, then left, then right... Just 3 turns".

I told the Lady, "I am so surprised you came outside, the way we look". She responded, "Sure I did, I don't care how you look, why don't you come move in over here, that house is vacant".

We got in the car after thanksgiving them and cried our eyeballs out.

Godly surely spoke in that moment. He let us know that he was waiting for us. He did not care how we looked, WE were 3 turns away, He had a mansion for us and more...wooo

Proverbs 4:7 (KJV) "Wisdom is the principal thing: therefore, get wisdom; and with all thy getting, get understanding".

The Takeaway

As long as blood is running warm in your veins you can repent and reconnect with God. You don't have to be in a church, you don't have to be at an altar. You don't have to sacrifice a fatted calf...you can stop right where you are and ask God to forgive you, and he is faithful to do it.

Prayer

Father God thank you for another Chance to say YES. YES, to your will, YES to your way. Thank you for allowing me to come back into the fold. You allowed me to make mistakes, and you still love me. I am so grateful Thank you, my name being written in the lamb's book of life. You alone are worthy! In Jesus' Name. Amen!

~TAKE AWAY NOTES~

Parable 22
Something is Stank in
Scriptures: Romans 16:19 (KJV)

***__Constipation__ is a condition in which you may have fewer than three bowel movements a week stools; stools that are hard, dry, or lumpy; stools that are difficult or painful to pass; or a feeling that not all stools have passed. (Webster Definition) You usually can take steps to prevent or relieve constipation.

Health care studies have found that a person should have a bowel movement after every meal and at very least, once daily...

So many of us are Constipated NATURALLY and SPIRITUALLY. It is imperative that we evacuate waste from our natural bodies. The body will (or is designed to) "eat the meat and spit out the bones" Romans 16:19, (KJV) by way of bowel movement; it will keep the good stuff and get rid of the part that is not needed or is harmful. Sometimes, however, the Natural Body requires assistance in this process by way of more "WATER" (the simple word of God). More "FRUIT", (the fruits of the spirit), diet change, exercise, and even MEDICATIONS and the DOCTORS intervention-but the WASTE must be evacuated, or the BODY will be Poisoned. APPLY THIS SPIRITUALLY.

Likewise, spiritually, it is important to get rid of the WASTE that hinders you from growing PROPERLY...malice, strife, jealousy, hatred, unforgiveness, gossiping, anger, depression, haughtiness, WHATEVER IT IS .... It must go.

IT IS POISONING YOU.... And it shows!

Your body will tell you when something is OFF.

The Takeaway

Somethings there were once needed for our growth and development are now NO LONGER needed and can cause problems and harm. Some people and things that were in our lives for maturation and growth are now hinderances to progress.

CHEW ON THAT~

Romans 16:19 (KJV) Everyone has heard about your obedience, so I rejoice because of you; but I want you to be wise about what is good, and innocent about what is evil.

Prayer

Dear Lord, thank you for allowing me to hear from you today. I pray that Your WORD harasses me in my daily comings and goings. Thank you, father, for feeding us naturally and spiritually. Thank you for the spiritual maturity to eat the meat and spit out the bones. Thank you for your words, the water, the milk, the meat, and the strong meat. Help us to continue to hunger and thirst for your word. I love you so much. Thank you for growth and the clean system. In Jesus' Name. Amen.

Parable 23

WRAPPED, TANGLED, TIED

Scripture: Luke 18:7 Hebrew 6:10 (KJV)

When Life Comes at you Hard-You Go Harder!

One thing that I have learned and KNOW to be true is that, when you get WRAPPED UP, TANGLED UP AND TIED UP in the things of God, He Will likewise, get WRAPPED UP, TANGLED UP AND TIED UP in your situation!

When you are stressed- Help your Neighbor, family, friend. Help them to talk, and or pray their things through. God will send someone to do that very thing for you.

When you are Broken-Help another gets mended, and our God will provide a mender for you.

When you are financially strapped-SOW A SEED, and God will have Blessings chase you down.

When you are ill-send Benevolence to another struggling in their body, and God will send his healing virtue to his child. Healing is Children's Bread.

When you are Sad-Bring a measure of JOY to another...And God will fill you with Joy!

I'm telling you: we can't make this stuff up. IT TAKES WORK, But IT WORKS!

*** Remember-Jesus gave and ministered out of his own need.

Luke 18:7 And shall not God avenge his own elect, which cry day and night unto him, though he bears long with them?

The Takeaway

When you get WRAPPED UP, TANGLED UP AND TIED UP in God's business, HE WILL do the exact same thing for you! He is not unrighteous to forget your labor of love and how you ministered to the saints and do minister.

Hebrew 6:10 (KJV)

Prayer

Dear Lord, thank you for allowing me to hear from you today. I pray that Your WORD harasses me in my daily comings and goings. Father God, please help me to keep my mind stayed on you. Amid all the hustle and Bustle, help me continue to keep you first! You are my strength and my guide. Help me to continue to love and show your love even when I am going through light afflictions myself. I love you and believe you to do it. In the name of Jesus. Amen.

~TAKE AWAY NOTES~

Parable 24

Abuse of Power

Juggernauts

Scripture: Leviticus 25:1 (KJV)

In this season, many of us have witnessed false motives, and manipulation amongst believers. Believers who have been in church for a long time, as well as those who have been in for a short period of time.

What is Manipulation?

Manipulate/Manipulation

Control of influence (a person or situation) cleverly, unfairly, or unscrupulously.

Vices of Manipulations vary from using finances, favors, close relationships, physical promises, and flirting, to name a few. MANIPULATION IS A SPIRIT!

Be so very careful to avoid operating in Manipulation.

Some of you are trying to use whatever influence you think you have to get someone to do what you want them to do because "you have their ear". Some of you try to manipulate your leaders, your subordinates, your family members, or anyone you think can provide you with a service, benefit, or something that will benefit you!

NO ONE is off limits for you.

You are abusing the POWER-you may or may not have, but it is the "motive" of trying to do it. And it is wrong whether you get the response you want or not. Be Careful My Friend.

STOP IT!

When you are manipulating and trying to alter the minds and behaviors of others. The bible says "Leviticus 25:1 (KJV) Do not take advantage of each other but fear your God. I am the Lord your God.

You are walking in a NASTY spirit! Some call it cunning, some call it sneaky, some call it Witchcraft...

Whatever you call it...Stop it!

Have an Amazing, Non-Manipulative Day!

The Takeaway

This time, it's short and sweet-Monitor your Motives, Monitor your Tactics. BE PURE. One beautiful thing is that, if this is you, you don't have to tell anyone. Just Change.

Prayer

Dear Lord, thank you for allowing me to hear from you today. I pray that Your WORD harasses me in my daily comings and goings. Dear Lord, please let me examine myself on a regular basis. Please help me to have pure motives and fair tactics when I am dealing with your people. Father, I want to be right, I want to be saved, and I want to be whole. I don't want to operate in the spirit of manipulation, but rather in Love and truthfulness. Thank you in advance Dear God, In the Name of Jesus, Amen.

Parable 25

Follow The Light, Not People

Psalms 37:37, Mark 4:19, Proverbs 14:12 (KJV)

My Friend and I were in the BIG APPLE-New York City, one weekend visiting, site seeing and eating a lot. During our visit we walked A LOT! We walked almost everywhere we went. As walked, we were ALWAYS behind other people walking, some from NYC and some not. One of the days we were walking, we were behind a group of women. When they moved-we moved when they stopped-we stopped. On one of the streets the traffic light indicated that we should cease from walking and wait, however, the ladies in front of us continued to walk. We were following them closely. I looked to the right and a huge gray suburban truck was inches away from me. I immediately looked UP at the light and saw that we did NOT have the right of way and should have STOPPED.

The Lord dropped in my spirit this thought about FOLLOWING HIM AND NOT PEOPLE. In this spiritual depiction, the Lord showed me that HE is the light that guides, "a lamp unto my feet and a light unto my path". He reminded me that it does not matter how busy life gets, and how many people affect my behavior. I am to keep my eyes on HIM for guidance. Even when other believers are behaving and living in a way that “seemeth right”; We are to incline our eyes and ears unto HIM for guidance. Scripture says in Proverbs 14:12 (KJV) “there is a way that seemeth right unto a man, but the end thereof are the ways of death…”

Psalm 37:37 (KJV)tells us to “Mark the perfect man and behold the upright, for the end of that man is peace. We can observe others for better ways of living and pleasing God, but ultimately, we are to FOLLOW CHRIST and seek HIM for guidance and direction.

The Takeaway

Continue to keep your eyes on the Lord. You can walk with People and talk with people. You can enjoy fellowship, but at the end of the day, and the beginning, you must submit to the Lord. Regardless of what the crowd is doing!

Prayer

Dear Lord, thank you for allowing me to hear from you today. I pray that Your WORD harasses me in my daily comings and goings. Father God in the name of Jesus, help us to follow you more closely that we ever have. Help us to discern the environments we are in and the people that we are hanging around and even those that are seemingly trying to connect with us. Help us to walk and follow you for miracles, signs, and exploits. We love you Lord and believe you to have your way in our lives. Thank you for forgiving us and keeping us, in Jesus’ name. Amen

Parable 26

Don't Abuse Grace

"Someone always knows."

Scripture Reference: Proverbs 15:3 (KJV)

"The eyes of the Lord are in every place beholding the Good and the Evil."

2 Examples

1). I was attempting to refinance my home a while back and was denied. Here is a small part of the backstory. I filed for bankruptcy back in 2011. After a bankruptcy, it is common for customers to "reaffirm "their home and "claim accountability" for the financial obligation. I had not reaffirmed my home after the discharge. Because I did not reaffirm the home upon discharge, the payments I make would not show up or report to my credit report.

When I realized that I could pay "whenever I got ready" instead of honoring the "PROMISE", I made via the promissory note, I did just that: PAID WHENEVER I Got ready!

My mindset was "it's not reporting to credit, so paying late will not go against me". Well, when I went to refinance my home. I COULD NOT! The finance company requires a full year of "ON TIME" payments to process a Refinance of a home.

When I heard this, I immediately thought "WHAT HAVE I DONE?".

2) I wanted to finance a New Central Heat and air unit through the electric company. This situation is likened to the story of the home finance in that payments were expected on a certain date. I paid the electric company when I felt like it, just in time to avoid having them cut me off. I did not honor the electric company, nor did I honor the principle of being a good steward. When I attempted to get a much-needed central heat and air; I COULD NOT. The electricity company required 12 months of successful on-time payments to be awarded these services.

The Takeaway

Both the Mortgage company and the Electric company expected me to pay my bill on time. I was fully aware of the contract, the rules, the obligations associated with services provided by these 2 companies. I made a conscious decision to Abuse Grace, and as a result of the blatant disregard, I forfeited some great opportunities. When we abuse grace, it may not report to a "proverbial" credit system, but it can severely hinder us from receiving other benefits and rewards that we could have been entitled to if we had operated with a different level of integrity and responsibility.

Prayer

Dear Lord, thank you for allowing me to hear from you today. I pray that Your WORD harasses me in my daily comings and goings. Lord Help us to operate with integrity, responsibility, and accountability. Please help us to budge our time, our money, and our priorities with the spirit of excellence. We want to please you and we want to be in a position to be blessed and to be a blessing. Help us walk in the way you would have us to go to be lenders and not borrowers! Thank you for your Grace, and we don't want to abuse it. We love you, in the name of Jesus. Amen

~TAKE AWAY NOTES~

Parable 27

Trash comes on Thursday.

Scripture Reference: 1Peter 5:7 (KJV)

A while back I was outside, and the trash truck rolled by. I looked back at my trash can and got disoriented because it was Wednesday. I stopped the trash truck on the way back through and asked, "did you all change trash day?". He replied, "no mam, I am dropping off cans for some customers who want 2 cans".

That scenario brought me to a thought...

TRASH COMES ON THURSDAY

I have a few people in my life who call me all the time with situations, and problems "TRASH", and I don't mind them coming to me for a listening ear and sometimes advise. However, I would become burdened down and overflowing with trash...mine and theirs.

When I saw that trash truck go by, and the man told me he was dropping off "additional cans" so more trash could be collected.

I thought "NOPE...ONE can-ONE day."

I will continue to be an ear, but only one day a week. I will not expand my capacity to hear and collect others trash.

The Takeaway

We can lend our ear and time to people but not to the point that it weighs us down and keeps us from performing and being all that we can be. Even at the airport, most airlines have a certain amount of baggage that an individual can bring on the plane. If that person brings too much, they are either charged, or they can't fly. All that weight hinders their "GOING FORTH". Encourage people to do the word.

1 Peter 5:7 (KJV) casting all your cares upon Him, for he careth for you. God won't fail and he can handle trash dumps all week long. Set boundaries and protect yourself.

Prayer

Dear Lord, thank you for allowing me to hear from you today. I pray that Your WORD harasses me in my daily comings and goings. Father, we thank you for leading us and guiding us. Giving us wisdom to assist when needed, but also being about to draw the line. Thank you for your words concerning us. Help us to be sweet and use wisdom to protect ourselves from being weighted down. You told us in your words to lay aside every weight and sin that so easily besets us. Thank you for your WORD. Glory.

In the name of Jesus, Amen!

Parable 28

Let me Take a Selfie

5 Browns

Scripture Reference: Psalm 139:23 (KJV)

I was invited to a women's luncheon some years ago. I had plenty of notice, but I could not come up with anything to speak about. There was no theme or topic. They told me "Just let the Lord use you". The day of the event, I got up and put on a brown printed dress, a brown shrug sweater, brown boots, and brown jewelry. In the house, all the browns looked the same shade, or at very least, similar. When I got outside, I noticed I had on clothing made up of 5 different shades of Brown that honestly did not blend well. I thought of the scene from Coach Carter. I almost went back into the house to change, but the Lord showed me what I was to speak of.

I spoke on how in MY LIGHT= I looked good. I was matching. My face was clear, and my makeup was applied flawlessly. My hair was in place, and I was ready to go. OHHHH but when I got in the Sunlight, or the SON-LIGHT, I had on 5 different non flattering BROWNS, I could see my pores in my face, my hair had flakes from gel, my eye liner was not applied correctly at all. I looked like a mess.

The Lord reminded me of a song I taught the youth choir, "while I'm down here praying, Lord searches my heart" and shines the spotlight from heaven on me. If you find anything in me that should not be. Take it out Lord.

Psalm 139:23 (KJV) Search me, God, and know my heart.

The Takeaway

A man or woman can look good in their own eyes, they can feel blameless and without error, but when they commit their lives to the examination under the light of God, they can see THEMSELVES CLEARLY. They can make necessary adjustments if they really desire to be pleasing to the Lord.

Prayer

Dear Lord, thank you for allowing me to hear from you today. I pray that Your WORD harasses me in my daily comings and goings. Father God, while I'm down here praying, Lord searches my heart and shine the spotlight from heaven on me. If you find anything in me that should not be. Take it out Lord. I want to please you. If you find anything in me that should not be. Take it out Lord. I want to please you. You said if our ways are pleasing, that we can ask whatever we will, and you would do it! Thank you for showing me-ME. I love you God in Jesus' Name. Amen.

~TAKE AWAY NOTES~

Parable 29

Let's Save the Baby

Real First Responders

Spiritual Reference: Luke 15:8-10 (KJV)

When I started my Ministry, Found Coin Outreach Ministries, The Lord had given me the scripture in Luke 15:8-10 (KJV) where the woman was cleaning her house to find one coin that had lost. When she found it, she went and told everyone because she was so happy the coin that was once lost had been found.

Luke 15:8-10 (KJV) Either what woman having ten pieces of silver, if she loses one piece, doth not light a candle, and sweep the house, and seek diligently till she finds it? And when she hath found it, she calleth her friends and her neighbors together, saying. Rejoice with me; for I have found the piece which I had lost. Likewise, I say unto you, there is joy in the presence of the angels of God over one sinner that repented.

Soon after the conception of the ministry, I organized an Intra denominational Prayer night at the local community center. Prior to the event, I had several different denominational leaders asking "religious" questions about the prayer night that was to come.

What should we wear?

Which church is hosting it?

Will there be music playing etc.

The Lord had brought to my remembrance a story to reference that I saw on CNN a few weeks prior. There was an earthquake in Nepal that was devastating. Buildings, stores, and homes were utterly demolished. People were missing and many were killed. Families were devastated while attempting to find their loved ones. In the headlines on the internet, first responders from all over came to join the various search parties. There were policemen, firemen, EMTS, paramedics and civilians moving debris and assisting strangers. These first responders had pulled out a big ole chunky baby from the rubble. The baby was alive, screaming, and unscathed-not a scratch anywhere. These responders were not fighting over who got there first or who was going to get credit, they were all trying to save the BABY.

In this example, the Lord had me to use our city as THE BABY! It did not matter which church gave more money, which pastor preached with most hoots; it did not matter who cut their hair, who wore pants, or who baptized in water or in Jesus' name ....

It mattered that WE CAME TOGETHER TO SAVE THE BABY!

The Takeaway

Everyone has something to offer the body of Christ, and we need each other to survive. For example. The paramedics may not have had the skills to remove rubble but were prepared to care for the baby in different ways if needed. EVERYONE WAS NEEDED. The purpose in coming together to assist the BABY is to realize who is "the BABY" in your life and you are a first responder.

Prayer

Dear Lord, thank you for allowing me to hear from you today. I pray that Your WORD harasses me in my daily comings and goings. Kind Father, thank you for allowing us to connect with other believers to respond, protect and save the proverbial babies in our lives. Give us witty inventions and strategies to be creative to assist where needed. Help us to be bold and strong with fighting the enemy. In the Powerful name of Jesus. Amen

~TAKE AWAY NOTES~

Parable 30
"IM CLOSED"
I am not ashamed of the Gospel of Christ
Scripture Reference: 2 Corinthian 6:17 James 3:10 Matthew 15:19 (KJV)

One Sunday after church I went to the local HOBBY LOBBY and found a sign on the front door in large, bold letters. CLOSED ON SUNDAY FOR THOSE WHO WANT TO WORSHIP GOD

I thought to myself "WOW, I LOVE THIS"

Seeing this BOLD stand for Christ stirred me up and provoked me to want to take a stronger stance as well. I'm determined to not only tell people that "IM CLOSED" to certain activities, but I'm going to tell them why "IM CLOSED".

"I'm CLOSED" to drinking alcohol because the Lord delivered me from alcoholism. 2 Corinthian 6:17 (KJV)- Tutu's reason.

"I'M CLOSED" to cursing or use of profanity because the word lets us know that blessings and cursing should not come out of the same mouth. James 3:10 (KJV)

"I'M CLOSED" to sexual perversion because I "WAS" and "WILL BE" again the wife of one husband and the word speaks against fornication and adultery. Matthew 15:19(KJV)

I chose these topics because they are common questions asked of me.

The Takeaway

In this season we are in and the climate of our environment, we as blood washed believers should not only decline certain things and activities, but also share why. It is a way of sharing our testimony, which the word declares "we are overcome by the blood of the lamb and the words of our testimony"
Revelation.
Decide what you are CLOSED to and take a strong stance. Whether you decide to be CLOSED to things due to spirituality concerns or Secular concerns... Take a Stance and BE CLOSED. There is a saying "If a person doesn't stand for something, they will fall for anything". As blood was believers we should stand for things of God. If God hates, it-we hate it If God loves it-we love it!

Prayer

Father God, we love you and believe you for the Word you have shared with us. We want to be stronger, bolder witness for you and your goodness. Give us boldness like never before to share and declare your word. Help us to create opportunities to give our testimony to others, that may be delivered as well. In the mighty name of Jesus, Amen!

Parable 31

Strength in the Storm

Community

I have a long row of pine trees that separate my yard from my neighbor's yard. One day a storm, consisting of strong winds, and heavy rains, came through my neighborhood and knocked over one of my humongous trees. This particular tree has been in my yard for over 20 years. The storm just blew it over like a twig.

So much revelation from this storm that I had to ask God, "How does a deeply rooted tree that appears to be IN THE WAY for a long time just blow down". The tree is fully grown, and robust in stature. How in the world does it just blow right OUT of the ground. Roots and all? The Lord ministered to me and prompted me to study trees and storms. I found that many of these older trees that appear to be FIRMLY rooted in the ground and secure in position, having long withstanding TERMITES eating at the roots, and parasites that damage the integrity of the tree's fibers. So, when a strong storm blows the tree, it can be partially or completely uprooted and broken in half. Galatians 5:7 (KJV) says, "You did run well, but something hindered you". The Song of Solomon 2:15 (KJV) declares "that the little foxes spoil the vine."

We know that unforgiveness, jealousy, bitterness, malice, and strife can destroy a person deeply, if not dealt with quickly, those things can take root and like the termite can eat us from the inside out.

Search your soul intentionally and often, "Lord while I'm down here praying shine the spotlight from heaven down on me."

The Takeaway

The tree fell over but did not hit the ground. There was a whole row of trees, a COMMUNITY, a FAMILY. The tree that was partially uprooted was hanging on by a few remaining roots, and the adjacent tree kept it from falling completely.

WE NEED EACH OTHER!

Prayer

Father God, we love you and believe you for the Word you have shared with us. We want to be stronger, bolder witness for you and your goodness. Father God, I love you and honor you. I need your strength to minister and serve my family as you would be pleased with. Please Lord, give me the strength to avoid discouragement when seeing things that are contrary to what you desire. Help me to hold fast to your will concerning me. Thank you for your strength and guidance concerning ministry and service.

In Jesus' Name Amen!

~TAKE AWAY NOTES~

~NOTE TO THE READER~

Thank you, Thank you, Thank you to all of you who purchased my special book of parables. Thank you to those of you who encouraged me and supported me along the way. I am so grateful for my journey and for the revelations that the Lord has given me and I'm looking forward to the next book of parables.

I pray that some of the parables and lessons resonated with your spirit, and I would love to hear from you.

I have already started working on volume 2. Continue to pray for me as I continue to serve the Lord in whatever capacity he decides to use me in.

Selah.

I LOVE you and there's nothing you can do about it!

DR. TUTU

Made in the USA
Columbia, SC
29 August 2024

41324397R00052